$\mathcal{T}o$

_____

$\mathcal{F}rom$

_____

ISBN 1-57748-886-5

Cover art: Debra Dixon

Scripture quotations marked NLT are taken from the *Holy Bible,* New Living Translation, copyright 1996. Used by permission of Tyndale House Publishers, Inc., Wheaton, Illinois 60189, USA. All rights reserved.

Published by Promise Press, an imprint of Barbour Publishing, Inc., P.O. Box 719, Uhrichsville, Ohio 44683
http://www.barbourbooks.com

Member of the
Evangelical Christian
Publishers Association

Printed in China.

GOD IS IN THE SMALL STUFF
for MEN

BRUCE & STAN

PROMISE
PRESS
An Imprint of Barbour Publishing

Contemplating God in nature often leaves us with a lopsided understanding of Him. We think about God as vast, immense, and impersonal. God created the universe, but He also created you. God knows you, God loves you, and God cares about the tiniest details of your life.

~

God is personal.
God is involved in our world.
And God has revealed
His nature to us.
All we have to do is
stop, look, and listen.

~

Religion is man's attempt to find God. The gospel is God's plan to reach man. Don't let religion stand in the way of your salvation.

God has given us His Word, His Son, and His Spirit. But the next step belongs to each of us. It's up to us to read God's Word, to believe in His Son, and to follow the guidance of the Holy Spirit.

~

One thing is for sure. You can know God's will. Although it may seem mysterious, there's really no mystery to it. If you know where to look, God's will is there. And if you listen carefully, God will speak to you in amazing ways.

God speaks through His Word, the Bible. God speaks through your own judgment and common sense. God speaks through the details of your life.

~

"God speaks in the language you know best— not through your ears but through your circumstances."

Oswald Chambers

You think your life is an accident? Not a chance. You're here for a reason. And what you do matters to God. Everything. Not just the stuff you do in church or Bible study, but in the everyday small stuff. That's where you'll find God's will most often.

~

Don't make plans and then ask for the Lord's approval. Ask God to direct your planning.

Remember that God's will is not so much a function of time and place as it is an attitude of the heart.

11

Realize your inadequacy without God and your sufficiency with God.

It's a fact of life. To grow in any area, you've got to do the little things over and over again. The principle of growth through detail is especially true in your spiritual life, yet people think that by praying once in a while (when they get in trouble), by going to church twice a year (on Christmas and Easter, of course), and by cracking open a Bible once in a blue moon, God will smile on them and give them blessing upon blessing.

~

The doorway to letting God into the details of your life—into your concerns and dreams—is time. We know this won't be easy. Many other voices will call out for your time and attention, and many of them are worthwhile. But if you want to hear the one Voice who will make all the difference in your life, you'll need to let God in. . .quietly.

~

Make an appointment with God
every day and then keep it
as if you were meeting with
the most important person
in the world.

～

The next time you go to church, don't look at the building or think about the schedule of events. Instead, look at the people. Appreciate them for who they are, what they need, and what they contribute to the church. Then think about yourself. What is your role in the church? Are you making a contribution to the overall health and fitness of the church?

~

Being a part of the church involves an interactive relationship between people with Christ as their common bond. With that definition, you can't "walk out of the church" on Sunday morning. You are part of the church all week long.

~

Science is not the enemy of God, and religion is not the enemy of science. After all, when God made the world, He made science possible.

People have chosen to focus on the creation rather than the Creator. That would be like seeing a beautiful painting and concluding that the artist had nothing to do with it, or that the artist really didn't matter. The same thing goes for God's creation. We are to appreciate it, protect it, and even manage it while preserving it. But we should never worship creation. All praise should go to the Creator, God Almighty.

So how do you find the satisfaction you've been looking for? The key is balance, consistency, and perseverance, all of which come from one thing and one thing only: *discipline.*

We want it all, and we want it now, whether it's an abundance of possessions or an abundance of simplicity. But nothing worthwhile comes quickly, and nothing worthwhile comes without discipline.

~

The secret behind most success stories? Discipline

It's easy to get caught in the trap of quick results when you focus on the results rather than the journey. The truth is, the joy is in the journey, in the daily discipline of growing in the details of your mind, body, and spirit. The only way to bring abundance to your life—the kind of abundance that gives you joy—is to bring discipline into your life.

~

*The first step
on the path to
commitment is
making up your mind.*

Satisfaction begins when comparison stops.

~

While the poor dream of having riches, the wealthy long for simplicity.

Simplicity doesn't take away from your life. A simpler lifestyle may actually *add* quality and contentment to your life. Simplicity doesn't mean poverty. Quite the opposite, when you identify those things and those people who are really important to you, your life takes on more meaning because you proactively choose to do those things that will increase the quality of your life. The net result is that your life is *richer,* not poorer.

Jesus made a simple statement about priorities when He said, "Make the kingdom of God your primary concern" (Matthew 6:33 NLT). What did He mean by this? Instead of being preoccupied with the details of your life, focus on God first. Trust Him to arrange your priorities. Trust Him to handle the small stuff.

If you find yourself putting your trust in money, intelligence, beauty, or success, remember that all these things come from God. Think about where your trust really belongs.

~

If you're an average person trying to get ahead in the world, contentment is probably the last thing you're striving for, yet there's a good chance that you long for it. Why? Because at its core, contentment is peace of mind. Contentment is happiness. The person who is content has little or no stress.

~

It's not only possible but desirable to be both content and ambitious. If your ambitions come from a desire to serve God, to help others, and to improve yourself so you will have a greater impact in your world, then the fulfillment of your ambitions will bring you much happiness and contentment.

~

"*I am an old man and have known a great many troubles, but most of them have never happened.*"

MARK TWAIN

~

Jesus asked the rhetorical question, "Can all your worries add a single moment to your life? Of course not" (Matthew 6:27 NLT). If anything, worries can and will take away from your life. Are you trying to arrange the details of your life so carefully that you are leaving God out of the process? Then you're probably worrying too much. You're relying on your own abilities, and you think you have a lot to lose if things don't turn out the way you want.

~

Anxiety is
short-lived if we give it to God.

~

*Prayer changes things;
worry changes nothing.*

Difficulties are opportunities for growth. If you try to avoid all trials, you are simply arresting your development.

~

When it comes to communication, there are two kinds of people in the world—those who love to hear others talk, and those who love to hear themselves talk (and we all know which kinds of people are more fun to be with).

~

Good communication skills begin with listening. Not only do you learn things about other people by listening, but you also make others feel important when you give them your full attention, complete with head nods and eye contact.

~

One of the last things Jesus said to His followers concerned leadership. He told them, "Those who are the greatest should take the lowest rank, and the leader should be like a servant" (Luke 22:26 NLT).

There you have it. The greatest leadership principle ever from the greatest leader ever. If you want to lead, you have to serve. If you want to be a great leader in God's Kingdom—the only one that counts for eternity—then you need to let God into the small stuff of your life as you faithfully serve others.

~

There's only one way to release money's grip on our lives, and that's to give up the idea of ownership. We've got to realize that God is the real owner of everything we have.

～

*Let money be
your servant,
not your master.*

The greatest cure for greed is generosity. It's also one of the most satisfying feelings in the world. But the only way to feel the satisfaction of true generosity is to give away something you value.

~

When it comes to generosity, ask yourself two questions. First, does your generosity come from your heart? A truly generous person gives out of love and compassion, not from a desire to impress others. Second, is your generosity productive? Remember, each time you give to those "in need," you are making an investment in God's resources. Invest wisely.

Laughing at ourselves gives us a more accurate sense of who we are. It breaks down barriers between others and us. It makes us more approachable. It projects a personality that is warm and friendly instead of rigid and stuffy. Laughter is like a magnet that attracts people. And if you can learn to laugh at yourself, you are guaranteed to have a lifetime of amusement.

~

*Our five senses are
incomplete without
the sixth—
a sense of humor.*

$\mathcal{The}$ truth is that we don't criticize others in order to help them. We criticize in order to make ourselves feel more important. We end up exaggerating the faults of others while excusing or ignoring our own shortcomings.

~

*If you make an effort
to overlook the little
faults in others,
they'll do
the same for you.*

There is one aspect of life which cannot be rushed—building a meaningful relationship with another person. You can make an acquaintance "on the spot," but a friendship won't happen instantaneously. And it doesn't develop overnight. It takes *time*. The most precious commodity of our "hurry up" society must be invested over the long term if you expect to have a friendship that is dependable and fulfilling.

Growing a friendship is not unlike growing a crop.

There has to be a season of planting: Time is spent in finding common interests.

There has to be a season of growing: You begin to appreciate each other's differences.

There is a lifelong season of harvest: The friendship proves to be a source of strength and encouragement to you.

The one love that will keep your marriage together. . .is *agape* love, which is the love that desires the best for the other person. This is unselfish love that seeks to give rather than take. This is love that takes work.

~

If loving your spouse unselfishly is a challenge for you, think about the way Jesus loves you. The Bible says that Jesus willingly "made himself nothing" in order to completely serve those He loved. And now He asks you to love your spouse in the same sacrificial way.

~

A Marriage can be a great investment that yields tremendous dividends, if you have the interest.

Be as enthusiastic to stay
married as you were
to get married.

~

*Loving your spouse
is not enough.
Learn how to
demonstrate your love.*

We have a suggestion for the perfect gift for your child. It is not easy to find, and it is terribly expensive, but we guarantee that it will last a lifetime and it will be your child's favorite. We're talking about your *time*.

Don't be misled by the myth of "quality time"—it is an admirable goal, but it should not be used as an excuse for missing "quantity time" with your child. Quality moments usually cannot be scheduled. They happen spontaneously, without warning, in circumstances you don't anticipate.

~

You already are an example for your teenager—whether you intend to be or not. The question is what *kind* of an example. Don't just *talk* to your teenager about life; show what you mean by how you live.

~

$\mathcal{D}o$ you want your teenager to have moral character? Then don't make promises unless you know you can keep them. Be just and equitable in establishing the rules of the household. Don't require any behavior from your child that you don't consistently exhibit yourself.

~

Once away from home, your child lives independently without any obligation of accountability to you. How do you convey your interest and concern without being accused of meddling? Here are a few suggestions:

Keep checking in without checking up.

Learn to listen instead of lecture.

Give advice only when asked.

Ask questions for the sake of praying, not prying.

~

Your love for your child doesn't diminish when he or she becomes an adult and leaves home. But the way in which you interact with your child will be drastically different.

Appreciate the difference. Your child certainly will.

~

Take a look at your own family. What kind of shape is it in? What are you doing to preserve and strengthen your family so your children and your children's children will be sure to hear the Good News message? God loves your family and He's counting on you to help preserve it for His glory.

~

Establish
family traditions
and faithfully
keep them.

~

Prefer the love of your family
over the praise of
acquaintances.

Seeing God in the "big things" of life is easy. The more difficult task—yet a challenge just as rewarding—is seeing God in our everyday, mundane activities. We need to have a "God consciousness" about our daily routine. We need a "divine perspective" about the details of life. We mustn't overlook God in the small stuff.

~

Before He created the universe ages ago, God knew all about us. We should not be surprised that He has ordered our days and is interactively involved in the events of our daily routine. Nothing escapes His notice. Nothing is too insignificant for His care. Live your life with an overwhelming sense that God is present in the details all around you. There will be no boring moments. Life will take on a new meaning when you begin to see God in the small stuff.

About the Authors

Bruce Bickel is a lawyer and **Stan Jantz** is a marketing consultant. But don't let those mundane occupations fool you. Bruce and Stan have collaborated on fifteen books, with combined sales of more than a million copies. Their passion is to present biblical truth in a clear, correct, and casual manner that encourages people to connect in a meaningful way with the living God.

Bruce and his wife, Cheryl, live in Fresno, California; they are active at Westmont College where Bruce is on the Board of Trustees and their two children attend. Stan and his wife, Karin, also live in Fresno; they are involved at Biola University where Stan is on the Board of Trustees and their two children attend.

Contact Bruce & Stan at:
www.bruceandstan.com

AVAILABLE
WHEREVER BOOKS
ARE SOLD

256 pages each; $12.99